MW01248743

# BLESSING

# &

# FAVOR

# DEVOTIONAL:

## 60 DAYS OF
## OVERFLOWING
## DEVOTION

*Susan J Perry*

# Copyright Page

*"GOD said it,*
*I didn't,*
*GOD told me to tell you!"*

*~ Susan J. Perry ~*

*Amos 3:7*
*Surely the Lord GOD will do nothing,*
*but he revealeth his secret unto his*
*servants the prophets.*

# INDEX OF CONTENTS

# DEVOTION

Our God brings us great hope for today, tomorrow and forever which is a very long time as we look into eternity, devoted to God the Father, God the Son and God the Holy Ghost who empowers us to carry on each day , and each year for the rest of our lives! God has put eternity in our hearts to look towards Him and keep our focus clearly aimed in the right direction! He has blessed and kept us all of our days! He has given us unmerited favor and for this kindness, we should be forever grateful!

Our devotion is in the Lord God Almighty who is and was and is to come!

*Revelation 1:8*
*I am Alpha and Omega, the beginning and the ending, saith the Lord, which is, and which was, and which is to come, the Almighty.*

# CENTRAL TRUTH

God is so good to us and we want to share a devotional with all of you on Blessings & Favor because it is an exciting way to live for the Lord! These are exciting times today as we see God move towards more and more of this glory as the world turns upside down in utter chaos!

Aren't we glad we serve a wonderful God? His name is even wonderful! (Isaiah 9:6) Let's declare Blessing & Favor scriptures aloud to enrich our lives exponentially today! For sixty days get a real grip on these benefits God offers us and enjoy this time together in Jesus mighty name, amen! Be exalted oh Lord, for you are great and greatly to be praised!

*Isaiah 9:6*
*For unto us a Child is born,*
*Unto us a Son is given;*
*And the government will be upon His shoulder.*
*And His name will be called*
***Wonderful***, *Counselor, Mighty God, Everlasting Father, Prince of Peace.*

*My cup runneth over and over...*
*In Memorial*

**Pastor Daniel J. Cyr**
**June 25, 1949 ~ July 31, 2021**

**Apostle Linda M. Cyr**
**March 19, 1951 ~ August 10, 2022**

*Resting In the Arms of Jesus*

*Isaiah 41:10*
*Fear not, for I am with you;*
*Be not dismayed, for I am your God.*
*I will strengthen you,*
*Yes, I will help you,*
*I will uphold you with My righteous right*
*hand.*

*Amen.*

*Apostle Linda & Pastor Daniel Cyr*
*Rest in Peace*
*We Love You!*

# A CUP OF BLESSING
# ON YOUR WAY!

# DAY ONE

*Psalm 5:12*
*For thou, LORD, wilt bless the righteous; with*
*favour wilt thou compass him as with a*
*shield.*

God is so good to bless us with favor
compassed around us like a shield! He calls us
righteous here. Let's declare it aloud:

**"We declare the LORD will bless the**
**righteous with favor compassed**
**around us as a shield!"**

IN JESUS MIGHTY NAME AMEN!

## OUR CUP RUNNETH OVER
## ONTO YOU!

# DAY TWO

*Proverbs 10:22*
*The blessing of the LORD, it maketh rich, and*
*he addeth no sorrow with it.*

Wow isn't that so good? The Lord will bless us
and we will never be the same and we will
never have sorrow because of it! Let's declare
it aloud today:

**"We declare the blessing of the Lord, it
makes us rich, and He adds no sorrow
with it!"**

IN JESUS MIGHTY NAME AMEN!

## COME HAVE A CUP OF COFFEE
## AND SWEET DEVOTION UNTO GOD!

# DAY THREE

*Deuteronomy 28:2*
*And all these blessings shall come on thee,*
*and overtake thee, if thou shalt hearken unto*
*the voice of the LORD thy God.*

God says if we listen to His voice or hearken
unto it, all these blessings will come upon and
overtake you! Let's declare it aloud today:

**"We declare as we hearken unto the
voice of the Lord, our blessings shall
come upon thee, (chase you down) and
overtake thee!"**

IN JESUS MIGHTY NAME AMEN!

## FILL MY CUP LORD
## WITH BLESSING & FAVOR!

# DAY FOUR

*Deuteronomy 11:27*
*A blessing, if ye obey the commandments of*
*the LORD your God, which I command you*
*this day:*

We must obey God's commandments in order
to be blessed, so let's do it readily... Let's
decree it aloud today:

**"We declare a blessing, if we obey the**
**commandments of the LORD**
**your God!"**

IN JESUS MIGHTY NAME AMEN!

# START YOUR DAY
## OUT RIGHT!

# DAY FIVE

*Psalm 3:8*
*Salvation belongeth unto the LORD:*
*thy blessing is upon thy people. Selah*

Salvation belongs to our Lord and He blesses us, His people with it! YAY! Let's declare it aloud today:

**"We declare salvation belongs to the LORD: The blessing is upon His people! Selah!"**

IN JESUS MIGHTY NAME AMEN!

## OUR CUP
## IS BLESSED!

# DAY SIX

*1 Corinthians 10:16*
*The cup of blessing which we bless, is it not the communion of the blood of Christ? The bread which we break, is it not the communion of the body of Christ?*

We all need a cup of blessing from the Lord! It is the communion we all may share with Him! Let's declare it aloud today:

**"We declare the cup of blessing is the communion of the blood of Christ; the bread which we break is the communion of the body of Christ!"**

IN JESUS MIGHTY NAME AMEN!

## WE HAVE A CUP OF INHERITANCE IN THE LORD!

# DAY SEVEN

*Psalm 16:5*
*The LORD is the portion of mine inheritance and of my cup: thou maintainest my lot.*

The Lord has given us an inheritance in Christ Jesus, this is a great blessing and He maintains it as well! Let's declare it aloud today:

**"We declare the LORD is the portion of our inheritance and our cup while He continues to maintain our lot!"**

IN JESUS MIGHTY NAME AMEN!

## OUR CUP IS
## TO BLESS MANY!

# DAY EIGHT

*Psalm 23:5*
*Thou preparest a table before me in the*
*presence of mine enemies: thou anointest my*
*head with oil; my cup runneth over.*

God blesses us with a seat at our enemies'
table! What a day that will be! Let's declare it
aloud today:

**"We declare God prepares a table**
**before us in the presence of our**
**enemies: You anoint our heads with**
**oil; our cup runs over and over and**
**over again blessing many!"**

IN JESUS MIGHTY NAME AMEN!

**OUR CUP IS NOT
JUST FOR ONE
BUT FOR MANY!**

# DAY NINE

*Psalm 116:13*
*I will take the cup of salvation, and call upon*
*the name of the LORD.*

How many know salvation unto the LORD is a big blessing? Let us drink of this cup! Let's declare it aloud today:

**"We declare we will take the cup of salvation, and call upon the name of the LORD readily!**

IN JESUS MIGHTY NAME AMEN!

**MY CUP CONTAINS
SALVATION TOO,
I AM BLESSED!**

# DAY TEN

*Psalm 106:4*
*Remember me, O LORD, with the favour that thou bearest unto thy people: O visit me with thy salvation;*

Remember us O LORD with your favor for this life and visit us with your salvation! Let's declare it aloud today:

**"We declare remember us O LORD with your favor for life and visit all of us with your salvation!"**

IN JESUS MIGHTY NAME AMEN!

# WE WILL TAKE OUR CUP OF FAVOR AND PROSPERITY!

# DAY ELEVEN

*Psalm 35:27*
*Let them shout for joy, and be glad,*
*that favour my righteous cause: yea, let them*
*say continually, Let the* LORD *be magnified,*
*which hath pleasure in the prosperity of his*
*servant.*

## "WE GOTTA SHOUT RIGHT HERE HALLELUJAH!"

We must shout for joy, and be glad, that favor is God's righteous cause: let us say continually, let the LORD be magnified, who has pleasure in the prosperity of His servant, meaning US! Let's declare it aloud today:

*"We declare we will shout for joy, and be glad that God's favor is His righteous cause: let us say continually, "Let the LORD be magnified, and may He have pleasure in the prosperity of His servant, that's US!"*

IN JESUS MIGHTY NAME AMEN!

# WE ARE BLESSED GOING IN AND COMING OUT!

# DAY TWELVE

*Psalm 41:11*
*By this I know that thou favourest me,*
*because mine enemy doth not triumph*
*over me.*

We are so glad God protects us from our enemies and gives us favor and they will never win! God takes us to victory! Let's declare it aloud today:

**"We declare by this I know God favors us because our enemies do not triumph over us, we are steadfast!"**

IN JESUS MIGHTY NAME AMEN!

## OUR CUP SURE
## TASTES GOOD!

# DAY THIRTEEN

*Psalm 102:13*
*Thou shalt arise, and have mercy upon Zion:*
*for the time to favour her, yea, the set time,*
*is come.*

God will have mercy on His church, for she is favored and her set time has come. Come LORD JESUS come! Let's declare it aloud today:

**"We declare God shall arise and have mercy on Zion (the church): for the time is to favor her, yes, the set time, is come!"**

IN JESUS MIGHTY NAME AMEN!

# ENTREAT GOD'S BLESSINGS & FAVOR WITH YOUR WHOLE HEART!

# DAY FOURTEEN

*Psalm 119:58*
*I intreated thy favour with my whole heart:*
*be merciful unto me according to thy word.*

En·treat
/inˈtrēt/
Verb

1. ask someone earnestly or anxiously to do something:

I asked earnestly for God's favor with my whole heart and He was merciful to me according to His word. Let's declare it aloud today:

***"We declare we earnestly asked of God's favor with our whole hearts and He was merciful unto us according to His word!"***

IN JESUS MIGHTY NAME AMEN!

# LORD GIVE US A
# FULL CUP OF UNDERSTANDING!

# DAY FIFTEEN

*Proverbs 3:4*
*So shalt thou find favour and good*
*understanding in the sight of God and man.*

We shall find it if we look for it, favor and good understanding with God and man. Let's declare it aloud today:

**"We declare we shall find favor and good understanding in the sight of God and man!"**

IN JESUS MIGHTY NAME AMEN!

## CHOOSE LIFE
## AND FIND FAVOR!

# DAY SIXTEEN

*Proverbs 8:35*
*For whoso findeth me findeth life, and shall*
*obtain favour of the LORD.*

I believe whosoever truly finds life, shall
obtain favor with the LORD! Let's declare it
aloud today:

**"We declare whosoever finds GOD,
shall find life, and shall obtain favor
with the LORD!"**

IN JESUS MIGHTY NAME AMEN!

# MY BEAUTIFUL CUP & SAUCER
## IS FOR YOU!

# DAY SEVENTEEN

*Genesis 12:2*
*And I will make of thee a great nation, and I*
*will bless thee, and make thy name great;*
*and thou shalt be a blessing:*

GOD promises to bless us and make us a great
nation! Imagine that? Let's declare it aloud
today:

***"We declare GOD will make us a great***
***nation, and will bless us and make our***
***name great, and we will bless others!"***

IN JESUS MIGHTY NAME AMEN!

# BLESS & SAVE OUR
# FAMILIES LORD!

# DAY EIGHTEEN

*Genesis 22:17*
*That in blessing I will bless thee, and in multiplying I will multiply thy seed as the stars of the heaven, and as the sand which is upon the sea shore; and thy seed shall possess the gate of his enemies;*

God blesses and multiplies us in oh so many ways as well as our seed! Let's declare it aloud today:

***"We declare that in blessing, God will bless us and multiply our seed as the stars of the heaven and as the sand upon the sea shore; and thy seed shall possess the gate of their enemies!"***

IN JESUS MIGHTY NAME AMEN!

WE ARE BLESSED WHEREVER WE GO,
LET'S HAVE A CUP OF TEA!

# DAY NINETEEN

*Deuteronomy 28:3*
*Blessed shalt thou be in the city,*
*and blessed shalt thou be in the field.*

We are blessed when we obey God; we shall be
blessed in the city and blessed out in the field!
Let's declare it aloud today:

**"We declare we are blessed in the city,**
**and blessed in the field as well!**
**Wherever we go, we are blessed!"**

IN JESUS MIGHTY NAME AMEN!

# GOD BLESSES
# OUR GENERATIONS!

# DAY TWENTY

*Deuteronomy 28:4*
*Blessed shall be the fruit of thy body, and the fruit of thy ground, and the fruit of thy cattle, the increase of thy kine, and the flocks of thy sheep.*

Everything about God's Kingdom is a blessing when we are obedient! Our whole lives shall reflect that! Let's declare it aloud today:

***"We declare we shall be blessed in the fruit of our body, and in the fruit of our ground and the fruit of our cattle and the increase of our flocks!"***

IN JESUS MIGHTY NAME AMEN!

TRY OUR FLAVOR,
IT'S FULL OF FAVOR
AND BLESSING!

# DAY TWENTY-ONE

*Deuteronomy 28:5*
*Blessed shall be thy basket and thy store.*

God blesses our basket and our store; these
are our goods surely! Let's declare it aloud
today:

**"We declare we are blessed in our
basket and our store by the LORD!"**

IN JESUS MIGHTY NAME AMEN!

OUR GOD IS SO GOOD
HE WILL GIVE YOU A
BIGGER CUP IF YOU NEED ONE!

# DAY TWENTY-TWO

*Deuteronomy 28:6*
*Blessed shalt thou be when thou comest in,*
*and blessed shalt thou be when thou*
*goest out.*

In and out blessings: We are blessed coming
and going when we love the Lord of glory!
Let's declare it aloud today:

***"We declare we are blessed when we
come in, and blessed shall we be going
out as the Lord determines!"***

IN JESUS MIGHTY NAME AMEN!

# FILL OUR CUP LORD,
## FILL IT UP!

# DAY TWENTY-THREE

*Ephesians 1:3*
*Blessed be the God and Father of our Lord*
*Jesus Christ, who hath blessed us with all*
*spiritual blessings in heavenly places*
*in Christ:*

Our Father in Heaven has blessed us with the
Lord Jesus Christ as Savior and with all
spiritual blessings in heavenly places in
Christ! Let's declare it aloud today:

**"We declare blessed be God the Father**
**of our Lord Jesus Christ, who has**
**blessed us with all spiritual blessings**
**in heavenly places in Christ!"**

IN JESUS MIGHTY NAME AMEN!

# THE CUP OF JESUS
# IS GREAT!

# DAY TWENTY-FOUR

*Psalm 133:3*
*As the dew of Hermon, and as the dew that*
*descended upon the mountains of Zion: for*
*there the LORD commanded the blessing, even*
*life for evermore.*

In unity we are blessed, Psalm 133 reflects this
and God commands the blessings for us! Let's
declare it aloud today:

**"We declare as the dew of Hermon as**
**the dew descended upon the mountains**
**of Zion, there the LORD commanded**
**the blessing, even life forevermore!"**

IN JESUS MIGHTY NAME AMEN!

## WITH THIS CUP WE
## MAY SIP THE BLESSINGS!

# DAY TWENTY-FIVE

*Hebrews 6:14*
*Saying, Surely blessing I will bless thee, and multiplying I will multiply thee.*

The Lord does bless and multiply us in His many ways! Let's declare it aloud today:

***"We declare saying surely blessing I will bless thee, and multiplying I will multiply thee!"***

IN JESUS MIGHTY NAME AMEN!

# LET OUR CUP OVERFLOW
# WITH HUMILTY!

# DAY TWENTY-SIX

*Luke 24:53*
*And were continually in the temple, praising*
*and blessing God. Amen.*

Our temple is full of praising and blessing
God, amen! Let's declare it aloud today:

**"We declare we were continually in the
temple, praising and blessing God.
Amen!"**

IN JESUS MIGHTY NAME AMEN!

# GOD'S CUP
## TASTES SO GOOD
## AND HE SHARES!

# DAY TWENTY-SEVEN

*Luke 6:28*
*Bless them that curse you, and pray for them*
*which despitefully use you.*

Sometimes we must turn the other cheek and
bless them that curse us or despitefully use us!
Let's declare it aloud today:

**"We declare we will bless those who**
**curse us, and pray for them which**
**despitefully use us!"**

IN JESUS MIGHTY NAME AMEN!

## MY CUP IS FULL
## OF JOY!

# DAY TWENTY-EIGHT

*Psalm 33:12*
*Blessed is the nation whose God is the L*ORD*;*
*and the people whom he hath chosen for his*
*own inheritance.*

Let's declare aloud, let America repent, and
will be saved and blessed today!

**"We declare the nation of the United
States of America whose GOD is the
LORD; will repent, be saved and
blessed to receive their inheritance!"**

IN JESUS MIGHTY NAME AMEN!

# FILL YOUR CUP
# WITH GOOD INGREDIENTS!

# DAY TWENTY-NINE

*John 15:11*
*I have told you this so that you will be filled*
*with my joy. Yes, your cup of joy will*
*overflow!*

Try drinking from this cup of joy; you will be
blessed and overflowing! Let's declare it
aloud today:

**"We declare we have been told this so**
**we will be filled with the Lord's joy; yes**
**our cup will overflow!"**

IN JESUS MIGHTY NAME AMEN!

# A CUP OF JOY
# CAN BE YOURS!

# DAY THIRTY

*John 16:24*
*You haven't tried this before, but begin now.*
*Ask, using my name, and you will receive,*
*and your cup of joy will overflow*

Asking in the Lord's name, we will receive now, and our cups of joy will overflow! Let's declare it aloud today:

**"We declare we haven't tried this before, but beginning now; ask using the Lord Jesus' name, and we will receive our cup of joy and it will overflow!"**

IN JESUS MIGHTY NAME AMEN!

## MY CUP IS SWEET
## WHEN IT INCLUDES JESUS!

# DAY THIRTY-ONE

*Psalm 34:1*
*I will bless the L*ORD *at all times: his praise*
*shall continually be in my mouth.*

We shall bless the Lord with our praise at all
times! Let's declare it aloud today:

**"We declare we will bless the LORD at
all times: His praise shall continually
be in our mouth!"**

IN JESUS MIGHTY NAME AMEN!

# EACH BLESSING IS FAVOR
# WITH GOD!

# DAY THIRTY-TWO

*Luke 6:38*
*Give, and it shall be given unto you; good measure, pressed down, and shaken together, and running over, shall men give into your bosom. For with the same measure that ye mete withal it shall be measured to you again.*

Glory to God we shall give and it shall be given unto us as scripted! Let's declare it aloud:

**"We declare when we give, it shall be given back unto us; good measure, pressed down, and shaken together, and running over, shall men give into your bosom; for with the same measure you mete, it shall be measured unto you again!"**

IN JESUS MIGHTY NAME AMEN!

# OUR PRAYER CUPS IN HEAVEN MUST BE FULL!

# DAY THIRTY-THREE

*Luke 2:52*
*And Jesus increased in wisdom and stature,*
*and in favour with God and man.*

Now this is our Lord and Savior Jesus who grew in stature, and favor with God and man in His time on earth. Let's declare it aloud today:

**"We declare Jesus, our Lord and Savior grew in stature and in favor with God and man during His time here on earth!"**

IN JESUS MIGHTY NAME AMEN!

# THE CHURCH HAS
# A FULL CUP OF BLESSING!

# DAY THIRTY-FOUR

*Acts 2:47*
*Praising God, and having favour with all the*
*people. And the Lord added to the church*
*daily such as should be saved.*

God is so good to us as He expands our
blessing and favor in the church as He adds
to it! Let's declare it aloud today:

**"We declare praising God, and having
favor with all the people as the Lord
added to the church daily such as
should be saved!"**

IN JESUS MIGHTY NAME AMEN!

# CUPPA, CUPPA
# EACH MORNING!

# DAY THIRTY-FIVE

*Psalm 30:5*
*His anger lasts a moment; his favor lasts for*
*life! Weeping may go on all night, but in the*
*morning there is joy.*

God's anger lasts but a moment, but His favor
lasts for a life-time! Let's declare it
aloud today:

**"We declare God's anger lasts a**
**moment, but His favor lasts for life;**
**weeping may endure for the night but**
**joy comes in the morning!"**

IN JESUS MIGHTY NAME AMEN!

## GOD HELPS LIFT YOUR CUP
## & GIVE YOU STRENGTH!

# DAY THIRTY-SIX

*Psalm 44:3*
*They did not conquer by their own strength*
*and skill, but by your mighty power and*
*because you smiled upon them and*
*favored them.*

We can not do anything in our own strength
or skill, but by your mighty power and favor
LORD, we will get the victory! Let's declare it
aloud today:

**"We declare we did not conquer by our
own strength or skill, but by God's
mighty power and because He smiled
upon us with favor!"**

IN JESUS MIGHTY NAME AMEN!

## SWEET IS THE CUP
## OF THE LORD!

# DAY THIRTY-SEVEN

*Romans 15:29*
*And I am sure that, when I come unto you, I*
*shall come in the fulness of the blessing of the*
*gospel of Christ.*

God sends us out with blessings of the gospel
of Jesus Christ! Let's declare it aloud today!

***"We declare we are sure we come unto***
***others as God gifts us in the fulness of***
***the blessing of the gospel of***
***Jesus Christ!"***

IN JESUS MIGHTY NAME AMEN!

# THERE ARE TREASURES
## IN THE CUP!

# DAY THIRTY-EIGHT

*Exodus 12:36*
*And the L*ORD *gave the people favour in the sight of the Egyptians, so that they lent unto them such things as they required. And they spoiled the Egyptians.*

The LORD gave His people favor with the Egyptians (the world) as they left captivity and spoiled them of much! Let's declare it aloud today:

**"The LORD will give His people favor leaving the world behind; taking all they can with them to spoil them of their worldly treasures!"**

IN JESUS MIGHTY NAME AMEN!

## OUR CUP HAS BEEN
## PRESERVED BY FAITH!

# DAY THIRTY-NINE

*Job 10:12*
*Thou hast granted me life and favour, and*
*thy visitation hath preserved my spirit.*

God has granted us life and favor and visited
us to preserve our spirit! Let's declare it aloud
today:

***"We declare God has granted us life***
***and favor, and visited us to preserve***
***our spirits!"***

IN JESUS MIGHTY NAME AMEN!

# WE ARE GIVEN A CUP OF RIGHTEOUSNESS BY GOD!

# DAY FORTY

*Job 33:26*
*He shall pray unto God, and he will*
*be favourable unto him: and he shall see his*
*face with joy: for he will render unto man*
*his righteousness*

God will be favorable with us when we pray to Him; and we shall see his face with joy and he will give man his righteousness! Let's declare it aloud today:

**"We declare when we pray to God, He will be favorable unto us; and we shall see His face with joy and He will give us His righteousness!"**

IN JESUS MIGHTY NAME AMEN!

# GOD HAS GIVEN US
# A CUP OF DOMINION!

# DAY FORTY-ONE

*Genesis 1:28*
*And God blessed them, and God said unto*
*them, Be fruitful, and multiply, and replenish*
*the earth, and subdue it: and have dominion*
*over the fish of the sea, and over the fowl of*
*the air, and over every living thing that*
*moveth upon the earth.*

God has blessed us and blessed our seed to
multiply as He did in the beginning! Let's
declare it aloud today:

***"We declare God has blessed us by***
***saying, "Be fruitful and multiply, and***
***replenish the earth, and subdue it, and***
***have dominion over every living thing***
***that moves upon the earth!"***

IN JESUS MIGHTY NAME AMEN!

## SEEK THE JOY OF THE LORD,
## HE WILL GIVE YOU STRENGTH!

# DAY FORTY-TWO

*Psalm 1:1*
*Blessed is the man that walketh not in the counsel of the ungodly, nor standeth in the way of sinners, nor sitteth in the seat of the scornful.*

We are blessed when we heed the Lord's counsel! Let's declare it aloud today:

**"We declare we are blessed because we do not seek ungodly counsel, or stand in the way of sinners nor sit in the seat of the scornful, it is the Lord who sends His counsel!"**

IN JESUS MIGHTY NAME AMEN!

# SHARE A CUP
# OF GOOD CHEER!

# DAY FORTY-THREE

*Psalm 2:12*
*Kiss the Son, lest he be angry, and ye perish*
*from the way, when his wrath is kindled but*
*a little. Blessed are all they that put their*
*trust in him.*

Kiss the Son of God, lest he be angry and we
perish from the way, when his wrath is
kindled but a little, instead be blessed by
trusting Him implicitly! Let's declare it
aloud today:

**"We declare we will kiss the Son of God
instead of anger Him and will be
blessed because we put our trust in
Him!"**

IN JESUS MIGHTY NAME AMEN!

## CLOSE YOUR EYES
## AND TAKE A SIP OF THIS CUP!

# DAY FORTY-FOUR

*Psalm 21:6*
*For thou hast made him most blessed for*
*ever: thou hast made him exceeding glad*
*with thy countenance.*

We are blessed by God for ever and He has
made us exceedingly glad with His
countenance! Let's declare it aloud today:

***"We declare we are blessed by God***
***forever and exceedingly glad with His***
***countenance!"***

IN JESUS MIGHTY NAME AMEN!

# BE CONFIDENT IN
# THE CUP YOU ARE DRINKING!

# DAY FORTY-FIVE

*Psalm 40:4*
*Blessed is that man that maketh the L*ORD *his trust, and respecteth not the proud, nor such as turn aside to lies.*

When a man trusts God, he is blessed and never respects the proud nor turns aside to their lies! Let's declare it aloud today:

**"We declare we are blessed when we trust the LORD, and respect NOT the proud, nor such as turn aside to their lies!"**

IN JESUS MIGHTY NAME AMEN!

# DRINK A CUP OF
# GOD'S MERCY TODAY!

# DAY FORTY-SIX

*1 Corinthians 10:21*
*Ye cannot drink the cup of the Lord, and*
*the cup of devils: ye cannot be partakers of*
*the Lord's table, and of the table of devils.*

Drink only the cup of the Lord because the
devil's cup is deadly poison but in God's cup
there is life and life abundant! Let's declare it
aloud today:

***We cannot drink the cup of the Lord,
and the cup of devils; we cannot
partake of both, there is no mixing, we
choose the Lord's!"***

IN JESUS MIGHTY NAME AMEN!

# PUT YOUR CUP IN GOD'S HANDS AND TRUST HIM!

# DAY FORTY-SEVEN

*Psalm 72:18*
*Blessed be the LORD God, the God of Israel,*
*who only doeth wondrous things.*

Blessed be the Lord God! He does such wonderful things! Let's declare it aloud today:

**"We declare blessed be the LORD God, the God of Israel, who only does wondrous things!"**

IN JESUS MIGHTY NAME AMEN!

## OUR CUP
## IS BORROWED!

# DAY FORTY-EIGHT

*Psalm 72:19*
*And blessed be his glorious name for ever:*
*and let the whole earth be filled with his*
*glory; Amen, and Amen.*

God's name is glorious and blessed! And the whole earth shall be filled with His glory! Let's declare it aloud today:

**"We declare blessed be God's name forever and let the whole earth be filled with His glory; Amen and Amen!"**

IN JESUS MIGHTY NAME AMEN!

# TEACH US FROM
# YOUR CUP LORD!

# DAY FORTY-NINE

*Psalm 84:5*
*Blessed is the man whose strength is in thee;*
*in whose heart are the ways of them.*

Our strength is in the LORD and we are
blessed! Let's declare it aloud today:

**"We declare we are blessed because
our strength is in the LORD, and our
hearts are in His ways!"**

IN JESUS MIGHTY NAME AMEN!

# GIVE US YOUR CUP
# OF CHASTISEMENT LORD!

# DAY FIFTY

*Psalm 94:12*
*Blessed is the man whom thou chastenest,*
*O L*ORD*, and teachest him out of thy law;*

We are blessed when God chastises us and teaches us His law! It is His Word! Let's declare it aloud today:

**"We declare we are blessed because The Lord will chastise us because He loves us, and will teach us His law!"**

IN JESUS MIGHTY NAME AMEN!

# YOUR CUP IS BIGGER
# THAN MINE!

# DAY FIFTY-ONE

*Mark 9:41*
*For whosoever shall give you a cup of water*
*to drink in my name, because ye belong to*
*Christ, verily I say unto you, he shall not lose*
*his reward.*

We are blessed to give a cup of water to
another, to drink in the name of Christ and we
will not lose our reward! Let's declare it
aloud today:

**"We declare for whosoever shall give a**
**cup of water to drink in God's name,**
**because we belong to Christ, we say to**
**you, you will not lose your reward!"**

IN JESUS MIGHTY NAME AMEN!

## DRINK THE CUP OF
## THE NEW TESTAMENT
## OF SHED BLOOD!

# DAY FIFTY-TWO

*Luke 22:20*
*Likewise also the cup after supper, saying,*
*This cup is the new testament in my blood,*
*which is shed for you.*

Drinking the cup of Jesus contains much more than our own cup, it's filled with saving grace! Let's declare it aloud today:

**"We declare likewise also the cup after supper, saying, This cup is the new testament in His blood, which is shed for us!"**

IN JESUS MIGHTY NAME AMEN!

## YOUR CUP IS
## FULL OF VICTORY!

# DAY FIFTY-THREE

*Psalm 103:1*
*Bless the LORD, O my soul: and all that is*
*within me, bless his holy name.*

We always bless the LORD from deep within
us; speak it out, *"Bless His holy name!"* Let's
declare it aloud today:

**"We declare bless the LORD, O my
soul: and all that is within me, bless
His holy name!"**

IN JESUS MIGHTY NAME AMEN!

## THE BLESSING OF THE LORD
## IS A FULL CUP!

# DAY FIFTY-FOUR

## The Abrahamic Blessing:

*Numbers 6:24-26*
*24 The LORD bless thee, and*
*keep thee:*
*25 The LORD make his face shine upon thee,*
*and be gracious unto thee:*
*26 The LORD lift up his countenance upon*
*thee, and give thee peace.*
*27 And they shall put my name upon the*
*children of Israel, and I will bless them.*

Let's declare it aloud today:

**"We declare the LORD will bless us,**
**and keep us;**

**The LORD will make His face to shine**
**upon us, and be gracious unto us: And**
**the LORD will lift up His countenance**
**upon us, and give us peace, and will**
**bless the children of Israel!"**

IN JESUS MIGHTY NAME AMEN!

# CAN YOU DRINK
# FROM MY CUP?

# DAY FIFTY-FIVE

*Psalm 24:5*
*He shall receive the blessing from the LORD,*
*and righteousness from the God of*
*his salvation.*

God will give us the blessing of the LORD in salvation. Let's declare it aloud today:

**"We declare we shall receive the blessing from the LORD, and righteousness from the God of our salvation!"**

IN JESUS MIGHTY NAME AMEN!

## GOD'S CUP OFFERED
## IS FULL OF GOOD NEWS!

# DAY FIFTY-SIX

*1 Peter 3:9*
*Not rendering evil for evil, or railing for*
*railing: but contrariwise blessing; knowing*
*that ye are thereunto called, that ye should*
*inherit a blessing.*

Never reciprocate evil for evil, but bless those
evil doers because the Lord has a blessing for
you! Let's declare it aloud today:

***"We declare not rendering evil for evil,***
***or railing for railing: but contrariwise***
***blessing; knowing we are called to***
***inherit the blessing!"***

IN JESUS MIGHTY NAME AMEN!

## STIR UP THE GIFTS INSIDE YOUR CUP!

# DAY FIFTY-SEVEN

*Psalm 119:65*
*Lord, I am overflowing with your blessings,*
*just as you promised.*

God's promises overflow upon us as we know
Him in salvation and enjoy the life He has
given for us! Let's declare it aloud today:

**"We declare, "Lord we are overflowing**
**with your blessings, just as you have**
**promised!"**

IN JESUS MIGHTY NAME AMEN!

# POUR US A CUP
# OF YOUR SPIRIT LORD!

# DAY FIFTY-EIGHT

*Psalm 145:18*
*The Lord is nigh unto all them that call upon*
*him, to all that call upon him in truth.*

We are blessed when we stay close unto the
LORD and call upon Him, His truth shall be
revealed! Let's declare it aloud today:

***"We declare the LORD is nigh unto all***
***of them that call upon Him; that call***
***upon Him in truth shall be blessed!"***

IN JESUS MIGHTY NAME AMEN!

# SHARE A CUP
# OF TRUTH WITH OTHERS!

# DAY FIFTY-NINE

*Romans 15:13*
*So I pray for you Gentiles that God who gives*
*you hope will keep you happy and full of*
*peace as you believe in him. I pray that God*
*will help you overflow with hope in him*
*through the Holy Spirit's power within you.*

As we pray, we hope for the best for everyone;
praying God will overflow hope in Him
through the Holy Spirit and power within.
Let's declare it aloud today:

**"We declare as we pray that God will**
**keep you happy and full of peace as**
**you believe more in Him; we pray that**
**God will overflow His hope unto you,**
**through the Holy Spirit's power with**
**in you!"**

IN JESUS MIGHTY NAME AMEN!

## HERE'S MY CUP LORD,
## FILL IT UP!

# DAY SIXTY

*Philippians 1:9*
*My prayer for you is that you*
*will overflow more and more with love for*
*others, and at the same time keep on growing*
*in spiritual knowledge and insight,*

Overflowing this cup God has given us is
tantamount to growing and maturing in the
Lord with the love for others with knowledge
and understanding for all! Let's declare it
aloud today:

**"We declare our prayer for you is that
your cup will overflow more and more
in the love for others, and continue to
grow and mature in the Spirit of the
LORD in knowledge and
understanding for all!"**

IN JESUS MIGHTY NAME AMEN!

# SALVATION PRAYER

## *Let's pray together...*

*Lord Jesus, I confess that I am a sinner and in need of salvation. I believe that You came to earth to seek and to save people who are lost in their sins, and I believe that You died on the cross as the substitute for my sins.*

*I believe that You took the punishment that I deserved for the sins that I have committed, and forgave me all my sins. I believe that You died for me and that You rose again from the dead, and that whoever believes in You will not perish but have everlasting life.*

*I trust in You and I place my faith in You. Thank You for dying for me, forgiving my sins, making me clean and covering me in Your own perfect righteousness. Thank You for all that You have done for me.*

*I receive You into my life as my Saviour and I choose to follow You and serve You all my life. Thank You for hearing my prayer,*

*Amen.*

# FINAL CONCLUSION

Our cup is a spiritual anomaly throughout the Bible! It represents our portion I would guess and even Jesus used this when in the Garden of Gethsemane when He asked Father if this cup could pass from Him because He was headed for death at the cross of crucifixion. In the Book of Matthew, Jesus said this in prayer:

*Matthew 26:39*
*He went a little farther and fell on His face, and prayed, saying, "O My Father, if it is possible, let this cup pass from Me; nevertheless, not as I will, but as You will."*

My conclusion is we all have a cup in this life and we have all got choices to make and we all hope they include Jesus. This salvation package offered by the Master will make your cup full to overflowing; if not you will find your cup empty and dry until you change your ways and take up the offer.

There are many benefits in your cup of salvation and I hope you have found your way to drink of this cup, a sweet offering from the LORD who:

*Psalm 68:19*
*Blessed be the Lord, Who daily loads us with benefits, The God of our salvation! Selah*

The offer of eternal life comes with every benefit package included in salvation. In this statement, we want us all to remember just one important thing:

*Jesus Christ is Lord!*

# AUTHOR'S CORNER

Susan J Perry born January 12, 1952 in Niskayuna, New York and resided in Schenectady, NY most of her early life. She graduated from Schalmont High School in Rotterdam, NY in 1970. She was saved to Jesus in the fall of 1998 in Houston, Texas where she lived for twenty-five years. She now lives and writes in Edgewater, Florida for fifteen years. She is married to John R Perry and they have 4 children in their blended marriage and 6 grandchildren who live all over the United States of America. They visit as much as they can.

She loves and serves her Lord Jesus Christ knowing only by His Spirit does she write and create page by page. Pure inspiration is so beautiful as the mornings run into nights and nights into mornings as she taps the keyboard on one finger quickly and as accurately as possible. She and her husband now publish books in *Simply This Publishing* and are having a great time doing so. Life is good for both of them. They give God all the praise, the honor and the glory for His loving ways. God is so good!

They have just started on children's books which are a new avenue for them and they hope it will work. They pray and ask God to direct their paths, and the funny thing is He does. God is in the blessing business and today is no different, God never changes, thankfully so.

They attend Edgewater Church of God in Edgewater, Florida with Bishop William T White and they love it there hearing the truth of God's Word. They are active in the church and are very thankful that they now serve locally, helping out as they are able.

Susan and her husband are ordained by Dr Frank and Karen Sumrall of Sumrall Global Ministries of Bristol, Virginia. Their life's call is in the Ministry of Helps to go into churches and help the Pastors wherever help is needed. They have an Aaron and Hur ministry of holding up the arms of the Pastors as they have need.

*Exodus 17:12*
*But Moses' hands became heavy; so they took a stone and put it under him, and he sat on it. And Aaron and Hur supported his hands, one on one side, and the other on the other side; and his hands were steady until the going down of the sun.*

Susan speaks at women's groups in churches when invited. She was teaching one of her books in Sunday night classes in her own church: "Lessons In Deliverance." What a time they all had too! They often find themselves in Clearwater or Dunedin, Florida on the west coast, three hours away, while they live on the east coast and love every minute of it. They take their books and have a product table to set up wherever they go. She and her husband go where the Lord sends them and they are glad to do it. God always provides.

*Psalm 100:2*
*Serve the LORD with gladness; come before his presence with joy.*

# CONTACT THE PERRYS

*1 Corinthians 14:3*
*But he who prophesies speaks edification and*
*exhortation and comfort to men*

All available on www.Amazon.com
Kindle Direct Publishing

## Simply This Publishing

John & Susan Perry
Edgewater, Florida

### Contact info:

Susan J Perry, Email:
susiebqt987p@yahoo.com
& Facebook; Simply This Publishing

John R Perry, Email: jperry8@bellsouth.net

### ALL BOOKS AVAILABLE ON
### AMAZON.COM

Books can also be ordered through bookstores
and big box stores if that is your preference.
There is always a way.

In Florida our books are available in:

**From My Library 2 URS**

**3510 S Nova Road, Suite # 107**

**Port Orange, Florida 32129**

**Proprietors: Samuel & Susan Titera**

# PERRY'S BOOK SHELF

## The Samaritan Woman Testifies
Kindle only: $9.95

## A Stone's Throw Away: A Woman Testifies
Paperback: $12.95 Kindle: $6.99

## The Persistent Widow Testifies
Paperback: $12.95 Kindle: $6.99

## The Woman Presenting the Alabaster Box Testifies
Paperback: $12.95 Kindle: $6.99

## Hidden in the Cleft of the Rock: A Woman Testifies
Paperback: $12.95 Kindle: $6.99

## Simply This: The World's Greatest Message
Paperback: $5.95 Kindle: $3.99

## Preach It Sister Girl!
Paperback: $9.95 Kindle: $5.99

## Daughters of Inheritance Testify
Paperback: $12.95 Kindle: $6.99

## ASK for WISDOM: The Safe Harbor of God
Hardcover $15.95 Paperback: $9.95
Kindle: $5.99

## Great Holes in Your Pockets: Recovering All!
Paperback: $9.95 Kindle $5.99

## This Project is Called: HONOR
Hardcover $15.95 Paperback: $12.95
Kindle: $5.99

## Our Experiences With ANGELS
Paperback $9.95 Kindle $5.99

## I AM A DUCK!
Paperback $9.95 Kindle $5.95

## The Double-Dip Blessings
Paperback $9.95 Kindle $5.99

## The Woman Touching the Hem of His Garment Testifies
Paperback $12.95 Kindle $6.99

### It's Never Too Late To Pray
Paperback $5.95 Kindle $2.99

### This is the Anemic Church
Paperback $9.95 Kindle $5.99

### There is a Witness!
Paperback $9.95 Kindle $5.99

### Heal Them ALL! The Children's Portion
Paperback $7.95 Kindle $3.99

### Ye Shall Serve God Upon This Mountain!
Paperback $9.95 Kindle $5.99

### Thanksgiving Is Best!
Paperback $7.95 Kindle $3.99

### The ABC'S of Perry
Paperback for kids $12.95

### LOVE is Surely the Way
Paperback $7.95 Kindle $3.99

### Lessons In Deliverance
Paperback $12.95 Kindle $6.99

### Cancel Cancer: And The Effects Thereof
Paperback $9.95 Kindle $5.99

**Royalty BELONGS To The Believer!**
Paperback $9.95 Kindle $5.99

**"Just When Did This Happen?"**
Paperback $9.95 Kindle $5.99

**I Declare Over You in Jesus Name**
Paperback $5.95 Kindle $3.99

**With Blessing & Favour**
**Will You Compass Me About!**
Paperback $9.95 Kindle $5.99

**Going Down The Barker Road**
**Missing...**
Paperback $9.95 Kindle $5.99

**Deception of Man: Sin Lies At The**
**Door**
Hard cover $15.95 Paperback $12.95
Kindle $6.99

**Beautiful Things: Out Of The Dust**
Paperback $9.95 Kindle $5.99

**In My Weakness God is Strong:**
**Declarations of Strength: 60 Days**
Paperback $15.95 Kindle $8.99

**The Year of 2022: A Miraculous Work!**
**60 Day Devotional**
Hardcover $15.95 Paperback $12.95
Kindle $6.99

**Love Endures Devotional:**
**60 Day Devotional**
Paperback $12.95 Kindle $6.99

**TRAUMA: The Doors Opened to a**
**Unique Spirit**
Hardcover $15.95 Paperback $12.95
Kindle $6.99

**Baking A Cake With GOD'S**
**Ingredients**
Hardcover $15.95 Paperback $12.95
Kindle $8.99

**The Holy Spirit Is Our Comforter**
Paperback $12.95 Kindle $6.99

**Be Anxious For Nothing But Pray**
**About Everything!**
Paperback $12.95 Kindle $6.99

**Pastor's Declaration Devotional**
Paperback $12.95 Kindle $6.99

**Because I Asked For Wisdom**
**Devotional**
Paperback $12.95 Kindle $6.99

**Our Devotional For America: In The Year of Our Lord**
Hardcover $15.95 Paperback $12.95
Kindle $6.99

**The ABC'S of GOD:**
**Knowing God More**
Paperback $5.95

**Psalm 139 is Mine!**
**The Presence and the Power of God**
Paperback $5.95

**Your Benefit Package In God**
Paperback $5.95

**Devotions In Prayer Unto God!**
**60 Day Devotional**
Paperback $9.95 Kindle $5.99

**Blessing & Favor Devotional:**
**60 Days Of Overflowing Devotion**
Paperback $12.95 Kindle $6.99

# RESOURCES

Wikipedia online research

Bible Gateway online Bible scripture research

The King James Study Bible

Various Bible Commentaries

Webster and Oxford Dictionary online
definitions

Black & White online free clipart

Amazon online website

No copyright infringement intended

Belief in Christ Jesus our Lord

And faith and prayer

# A Good Friend

## (8/10/2022)

A good friend has left us today,
Headed home to Jesus,
Open arms to stay!
Death did not part us,
Our spirits will remain;
We must know Jesus,
Cleansed in the Blood of the stain.

O how can we miss her,
Another gone so far away?
Heaven's gates opened wide,
And accepted her, this beloved mate.
We know it is forever,
She will be never again late.
Her troubles are over,
Her life now filled with sweet taste,
Heaven is her home now,
Going forward we hope to see her,
We too may have to wait.

The world will never be the same,
I long to hear her say, "FIRE!"
Just one more time...
And knowing, now she is delivered to
the arms,
Of all those who love her,
And,
No more waiting for that ole pearly gate.

I know Jesus smiled and spoke softly in
her ear,

*"Well done thou good and faithful servant,*
*You have come home,*
*There is nothing more to fear..."*

*Apostle Linda M. Cyr*

# CUPPA CUPPA CAKE RECIPE

## INGREDIENTS:

1 Cup Rising Flour

1 Cup Sugar

1 Can Fruit Cocktail With Juice

Softened Butter, For Pan

Unsweetened Whipped Cream, For
Serving

(Or Vanilla Ice Cream)

**************************

## DIRECTIONS:

Preheat oven to 350 degrees

Grease 8" square baking dish with
butter

Stir together flour, sugar, and fruit
cocktail with juice until combined

Pour into buttered pan and bake until
warm and bubbly
(45 minutes)

Serve warm with unsweetened whipped
cream

Or vanilla ice cream

Yields 12 servings

Made in the USA
Columbia, SC
04 September 2022

66440329R00083